TINY SCIENCE

ATOMS AND MOLECULES

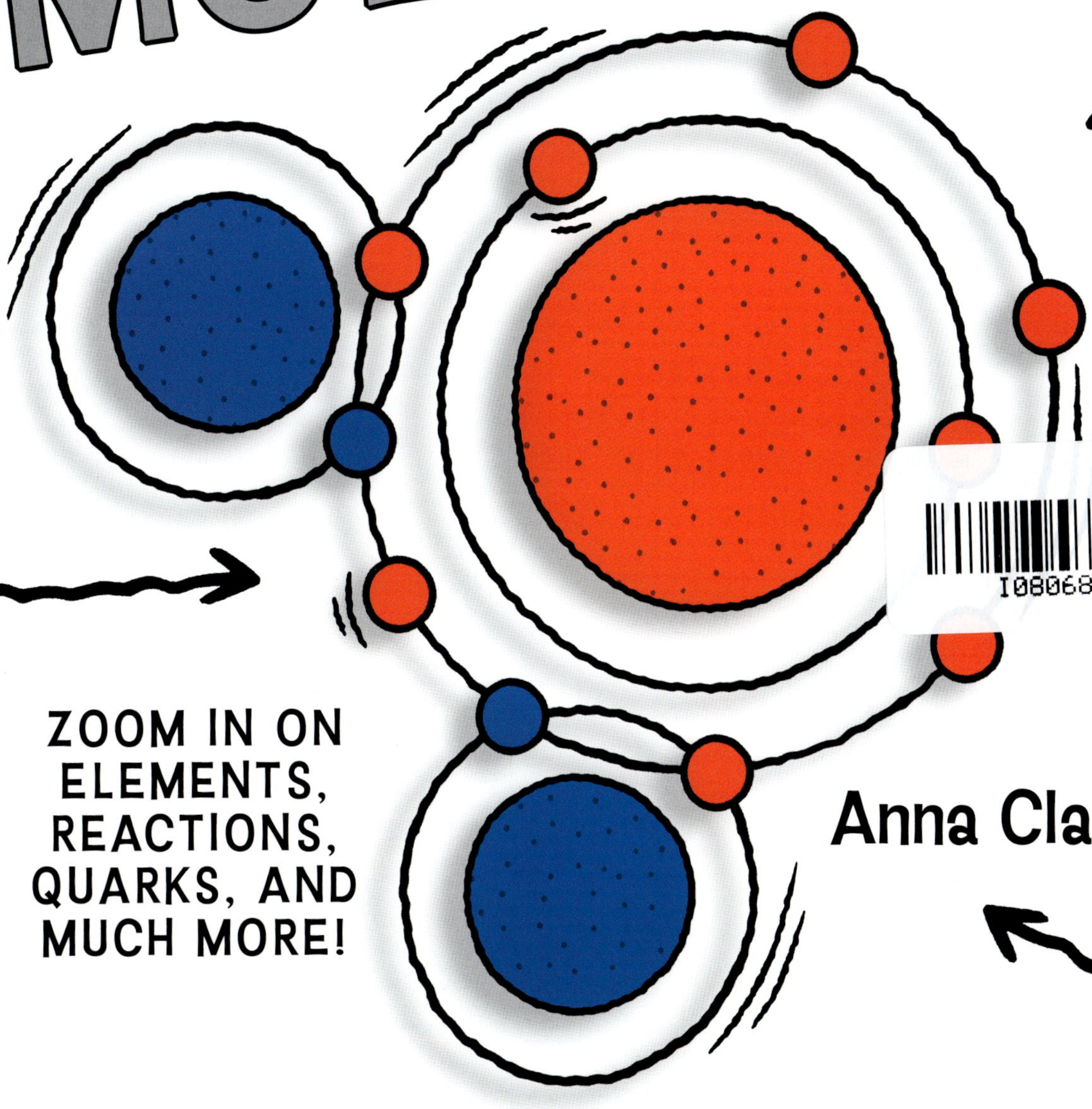

ZOOM IN ON ELEMENTS, REACTIONS, QUARKS, AND MUCH MORE!

Anna Claybourne

Gareth Stevens PUBLISHING

Please visit our website, www.garethstevens.com. For a free color catalog of all our high-quality books, call toll free 1-800-542-2595 or fax 1-877-542-2596.

Published in 2025 by
Gareth Stevens Publishing
2544 Clinton St.
Buffalo, NY 14224

First published in Great Britain in 2022 by Wayland

Editor:
Grace Glendinning

Design and illustrations:
Matt Lilly

Cover design:
Matt Lilly

Cataloging-in-Publication Data

Names: Claybourne, Anna.
Title: Atoms and molecules / Anna Claybourne.
Description: Buffalo, NY : Gareth Stevens Publishing, 2025. | Series: Tiny science | Includes glossary and index.
Identifiers: ISBN 9781538294055 (pbk.) | ISBN 9781538294062 (library bound) | ISBN 9781538294079 (ebook)
Subjects: LCSH: Atoms--Juvenile literature. | Molecules--Juvenile literature.
Classification: LCC QC173.16 C54 2025 | DDC 530.4--dc23

Alamy: Andrew Dunn 6t.
Dreamstime: Natalia Rumyantseva 18c, 20t.
iStock: Duntaro 11b; Evgeny Zhigalov 25tr.
Science Photo Library: Biofotos Associates 10cr; Andrew Brookes/National Physical Lab 25tl; IBM Research 25tl, 25b; R3F 14t, 23b; Sheila Terry 18bl.
Shutterstock: Alexyz3d 21b;Vladimir Arndt 13c; AvDe 17b; Cherkas 10tl; Daisy Daisy 6b;DKN0049 12br; Everett Collection 19tl;Fosin 7t; Richard Julliart 26; StudioMolekuul 12bl; Anusorn Nakdee 17t; Oneinchpunch 13br; Simon Pikous 15tc;1Matthew Rushmore 15tr.
© 2021 The Pennsylvania State University/CCA 4.0 22b.
Wikimedia Commons/PD 22c, 23t.

Printed in the United States of America

CPSIA compliance information: Batch #CSGS25: For further information contact Gareth Stevens at 1-800-542-2595.

Contents

What's everything made of?

We're surrounded by stuff!
Or, as scientists like to call it, MATTER.

But the question is ... **What IS matter?**

Tiny bits!

More than 2,500 years ago, several people in ancient Greece and ancient India came up with the same idea. They thought everything must be made up of tiny parts, each one too small to see.

Ancient Greek thinker Democritus called these parts "atomos," or atoms, meaning "uncuttable."* In other words, Democritus said that an atom is the smallest thing there is and can't be cut in two.

So, were they right?

KIND OF!

We now know that matter really is made up of tiny units – and we still call them atoms!

*But as for the "uncuttable" part, see pages 20–21.

What are they like?

Atoms are a bit like tiny balls. There are over 100 different types of atoms. Here are just a few of them:

Then ... what are molecules?

Atoms can exist on their own. But they can also join up to make bigger units, called **MOLECULES**.

A glass of water

Many everyday materials are made of molecules, which are all made up of different types of atoms.

Teeny tiny!

Atoms are small. Really, **REALLY** small!

A typical atom is about 0.1 nanometers (nm) across.
1 nanometer is 1 millionth of a millimeter (mm).

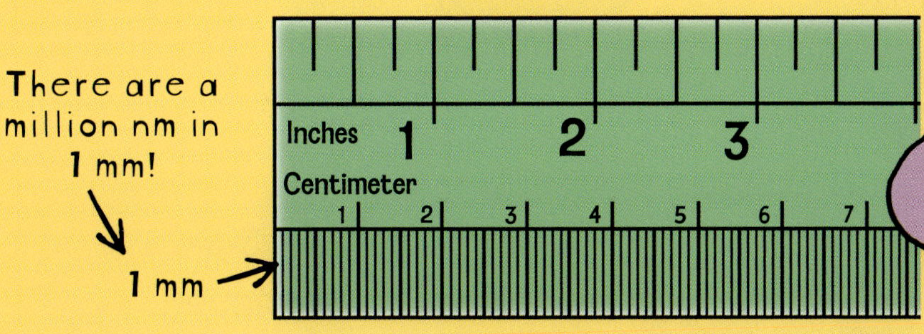

And an average glass of water contains about
30,000,000,000,000,000,000,000,000,000
(or 30 trillion trillion) atoms!

What are atoms really like?

Turn the page for a closer look!

Atoms in close-up

Just one page ago, we said atoms were like balls. But it's actually a bit more complicated than that!

Under the microscope

Today, powerful microscopes can capture images of real atoms. In this picture, the atoms do look like balls.

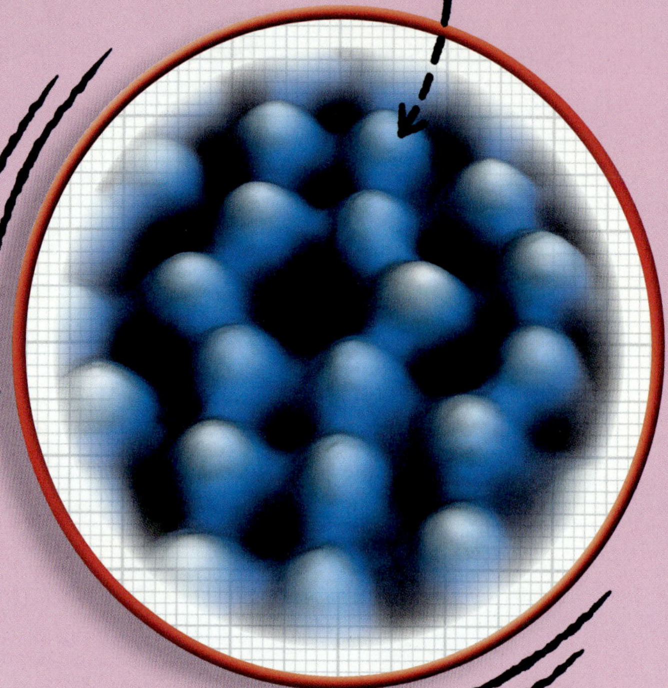

Real silicon atoms in a silicon chip, used to make computers

Atom diagrams

In illustrated diagrams, atoms look like balls too.

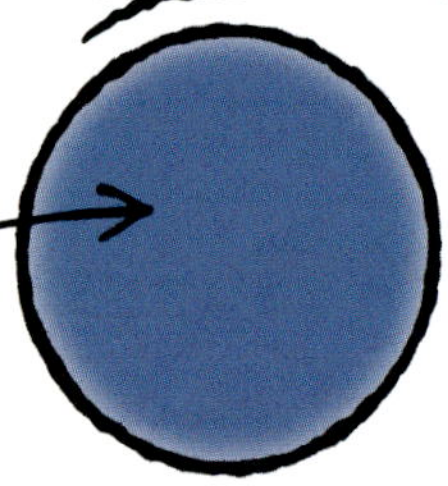

Silicon atom

Molecule made of silicon and hydrogen atoms

And you can get 3-D models with ball-shaped atoms and sticks to join them together into molecules.

Inside an atom

But an atom is not just a smooth, round ball. It has several different parts.

Here are the parts of a helium atom, for example.

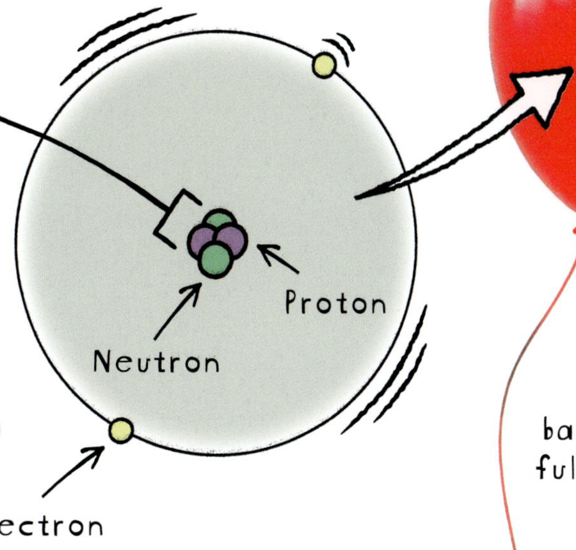

In the middle is a tiny nucleus.

It's made up of even smaller parts called neutrons and protons.

Even tinier parts, called electrons, zoom around the nucleus.

They whiz around so fast, it's as if they are in many places at once. This gives the atom its round shape.

Helium balloons are full of helium atoms!

The parts that make up an atom are called **subatomic particles**.

Empty space

This means that an atom is mostly made of ... **NOTHING!** If an atom was the size of a soccer stadium, the nucleus would be the size of a pea. Each electron would be smaller than a grain of sand. The rest is empty space!

Tennis ball

If you squashed all the empty space out of all the atoms in every person in the world, we'd all fit inside a tennis ball!

Making molecules

Molecules are made up of atoms joined together. But why do atoms do that?

Shall we share?

When atoms join, or bond, they are usually sharing or swapping their electrons. Some types of atoms naturally bond together, depending on how many electrons they have to begin with.

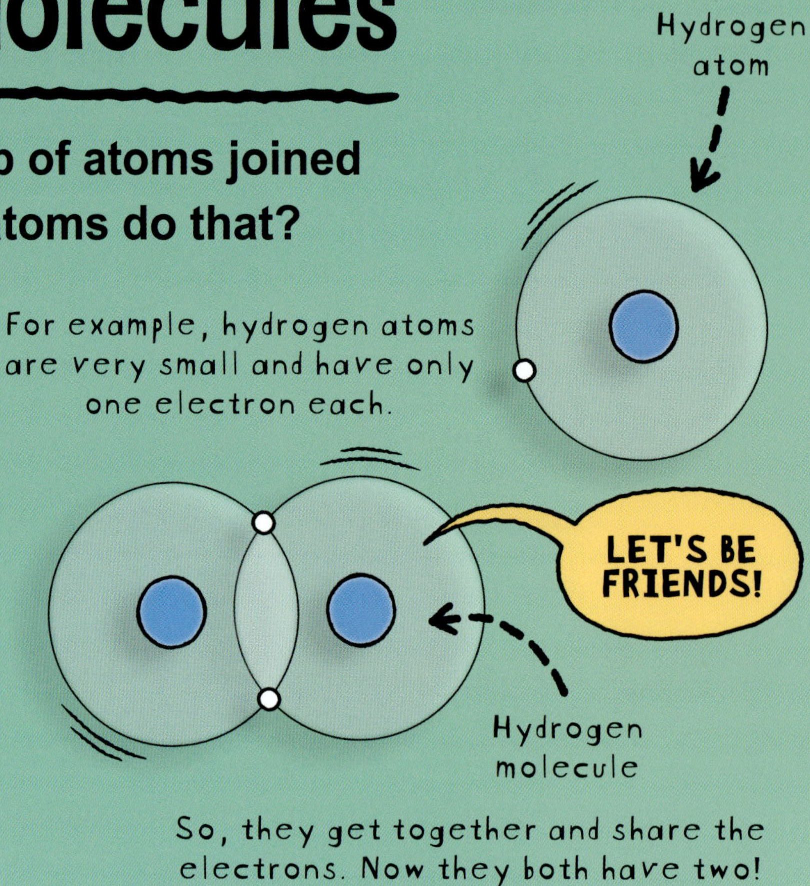

Billions of bonds

This is just the simplest type of molecule. There are millions more, made up of all kinds of combinations of different atoms. Some just have two or three atoms, while some have hundreds or even thousands.

There are thousands of different molecules all around us.

Water

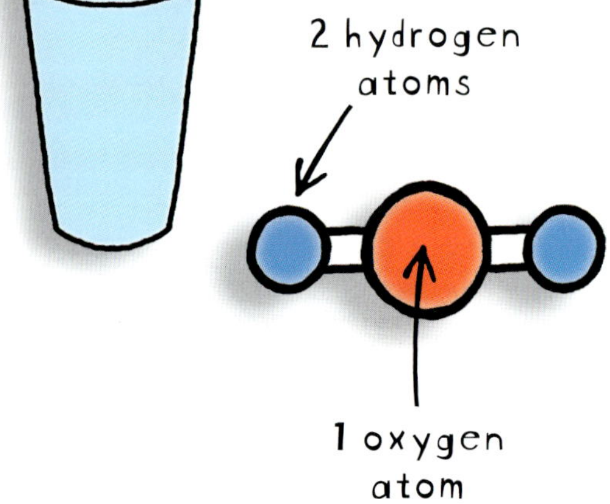

Carbon dioxide

Methane gas

Found in gas cookers, rocket fuel, and farts!

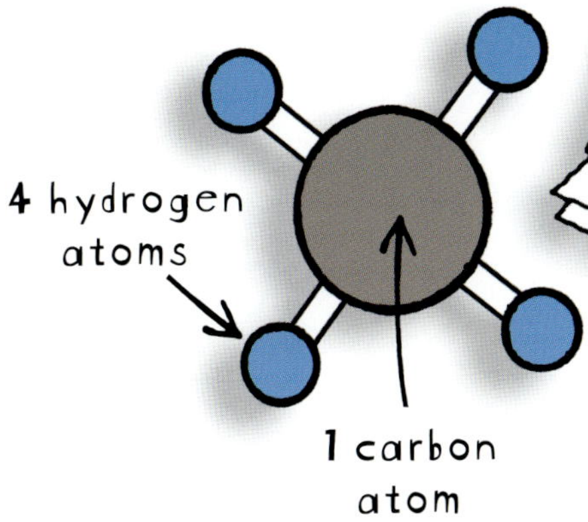

Caffeine

found in coffee

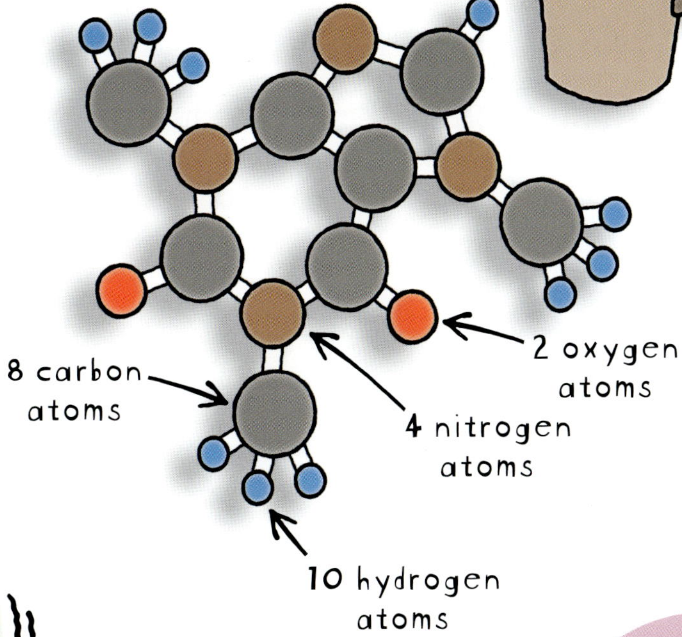

Call it chemistry!

If you've ever wondered what chemistry is – this is it! It's simply the science of how atoms bond to make different kinds of matter.

Edible molecule models

Molecule models show how atoms fit together. Try making your own, then eat the atoms afterward!

BLOOP BLOOP! SAFETY WARNING!

Make sure you ask an adult to do this with you.

See if you can make some of the molecules on this page.

Use small, roundish foods like grapes, berries, or marshmallows for the atoms. Use pieces of uncooked spaghetti or wooden cocktail sticks to join them together.

It's elementary!

An element is a pure substance that's made of just one type of atom.

Each type of atom has its own element.

For example, gold is a type of atom ...

... and gold is an element, made of just gold atoms and nothing else.

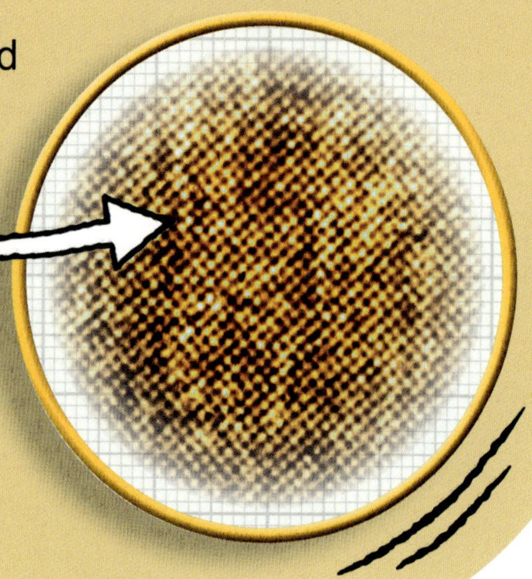

Under the microscope

This microscope photo shows a piece of gold so close up, you can see its atoms.

Elements are everywhere!

Many elements are normal, everyday substances.

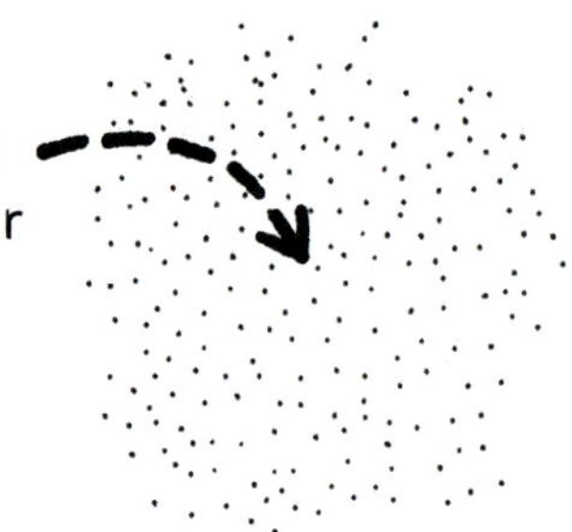

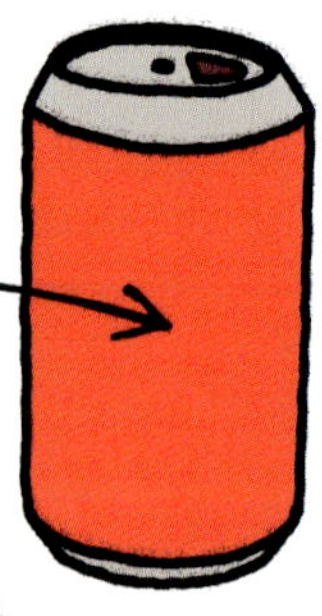

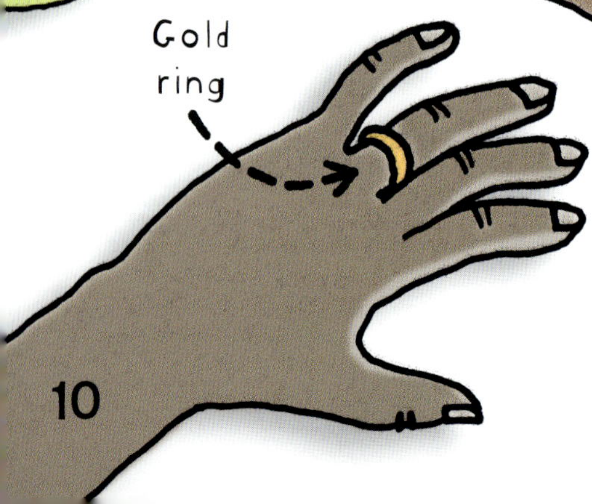

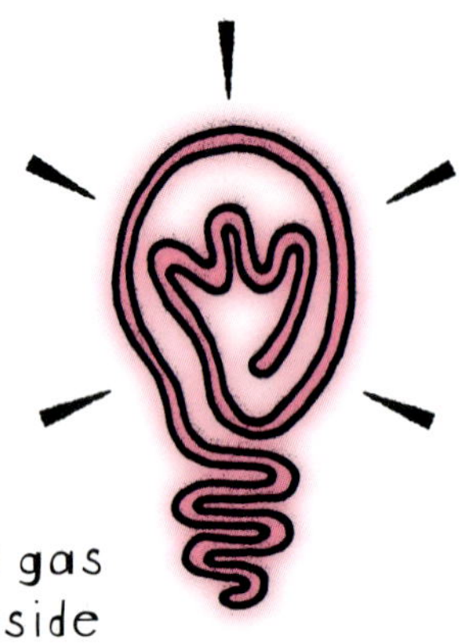

So, what makes elements different from one another?

The answer is how many teeny-weeny protons there are clustered in an atom's nucleus.

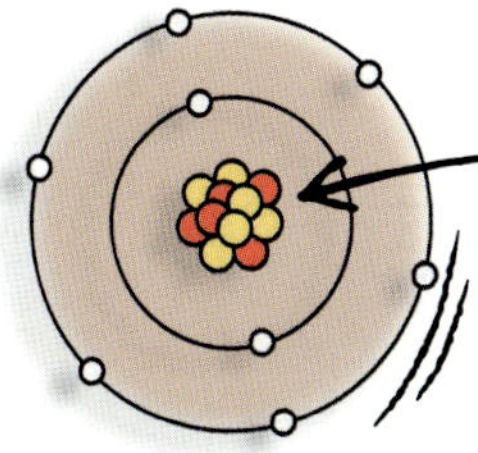

For example, oxygen atoms have eight protons, forming the nucleus with the eight neutrons.

Gold atoms have a whopping 79 protons.

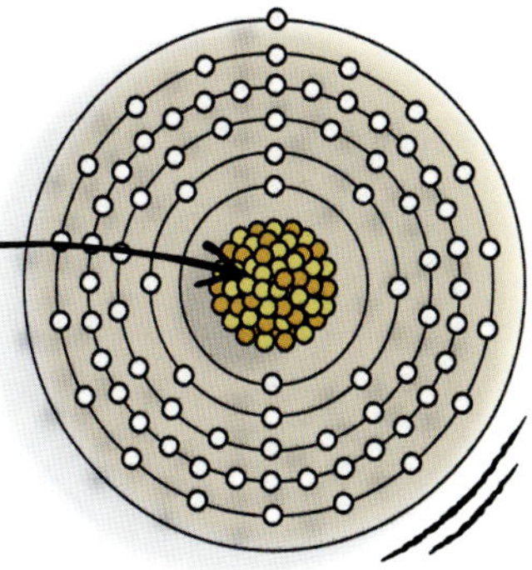

A typical atom has the same number of electrons as protons. When an atom has more than two electrons, they're arranged in layers, known as shells.

All the elements

In fact, each atom has a number, from 1, which is hydrogen, all the way up to 118, which is a rare element called oganesson.

Each element in the table has:

An atomic number - the number of protons

An atomic mass - the average number of protons and neutrons together

A symbol made of one or two letters - the symbol for oxygen is O

Scientists arrange elements in a table called the Periodic Table of the Elements.

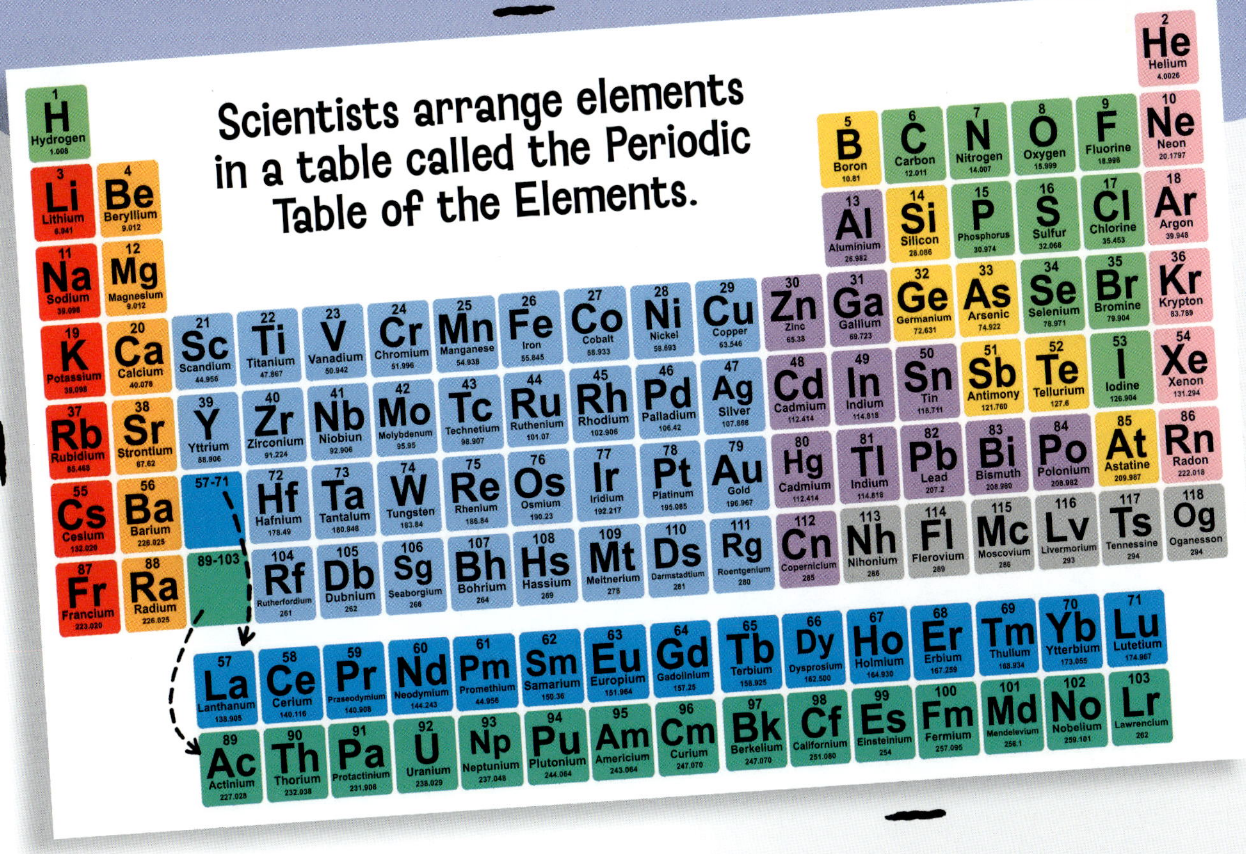

Millions of materials

Our world is made up of MILLIONS of different materials and substances. Look around and you'll see countless different examples ...

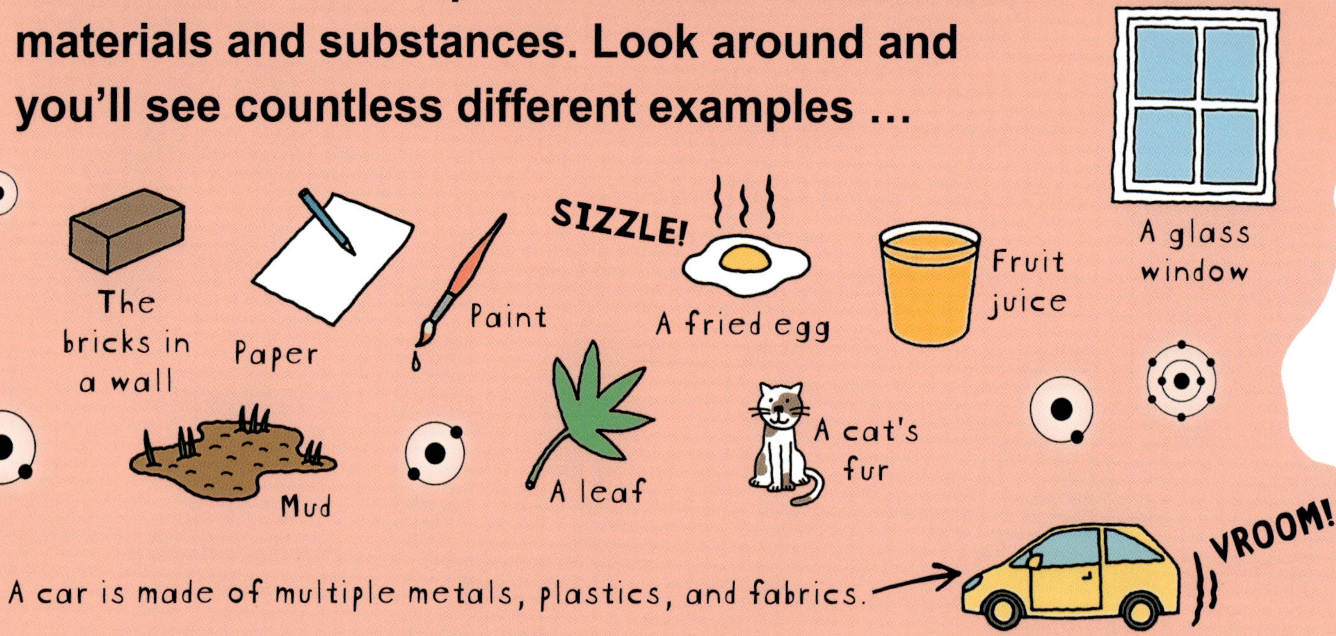

Yet if you could look closely enough, you'd see that **ALL** of them are made of the same 100 or so types of tiny atoms – the building blocks of all matter.

How do they do it?

Atoms make all these different materials in **three main ways**.

The simplest are the **elements**, made of one type of atom.

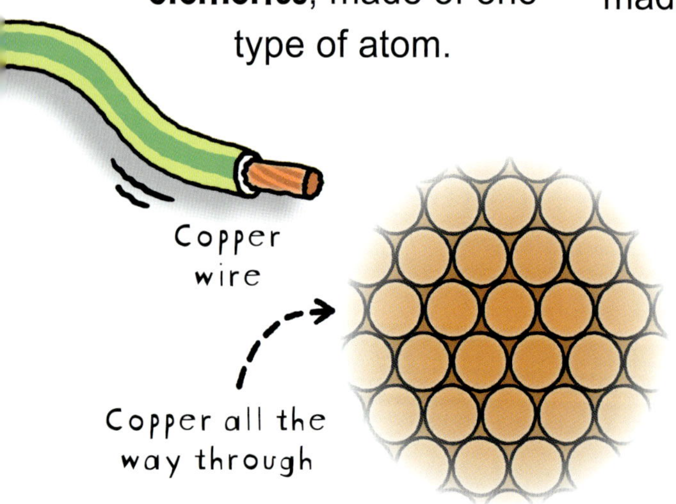

Then there are the **compounds**, made of one type of molecule.

Table salt is a compound.

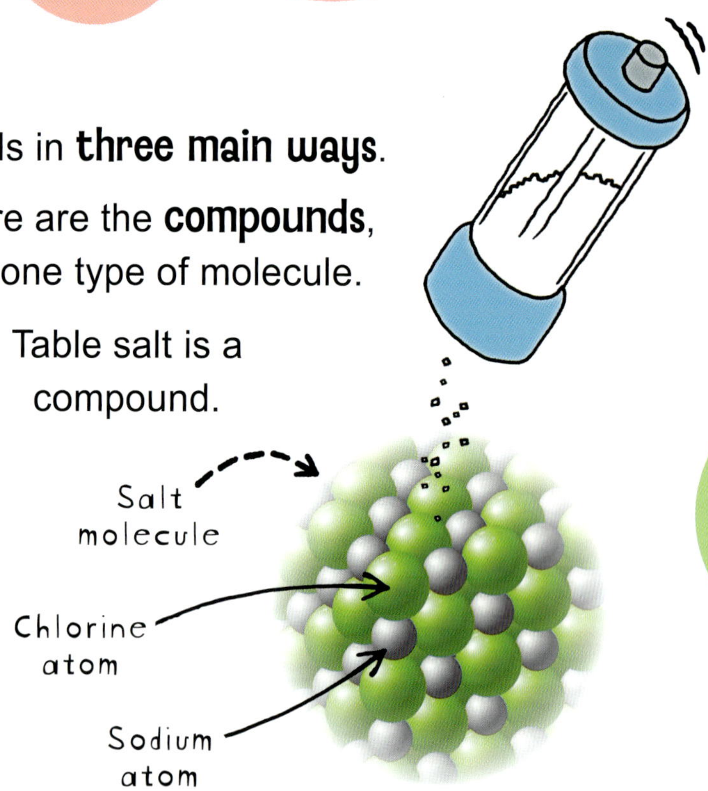

Anything made of one type of molecule is a compound:

Water is a compound.

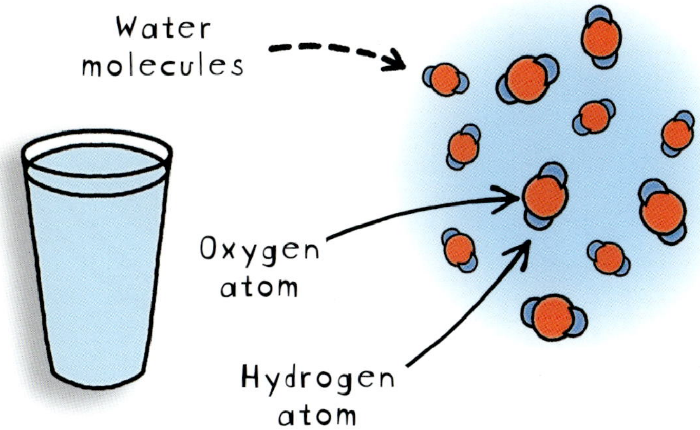

Carbon dioxide gas is a compound.

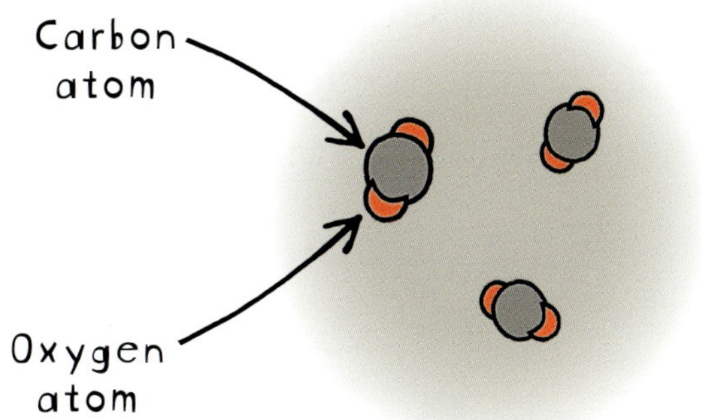

Mix it up!

Finally, a LOT of the things around us are not elements or compounds, but **mixtures**.

A typical rock, for example, could be a mixture of several compounds and elements.

Mixed-up world

Considering how big and complicated the world is, it's not surprising that many materials are mixtures!

Living things are mixtures, and so are soil, air, and seawater.

A book is a mixture of inks, paper, and cardboard or card stock.

Most foods are mixtures.

Party outfit!

The sparkly fabric in this jacket could be a mixture of:

Shiny metal fibers

Polyester, a type of plastic molecule

Cotton, made of cellulose molecules

Dye, made of several different chemicals

BOOM!

If you drop a lump of the element sodium into a bowl of water, what do you get?

Fizz ... sputter ...

BANG!

DON'T try this at home!

What happened?

Sometimes, when different substances meet, their atoms rearrange themselves and form new molecules. It's called a chemical reaction.

With sodium and water, the reaction is very fast and gives out lots of energy – an explosion, in other words! Here you can see how the molecules change and the atoms swap around:

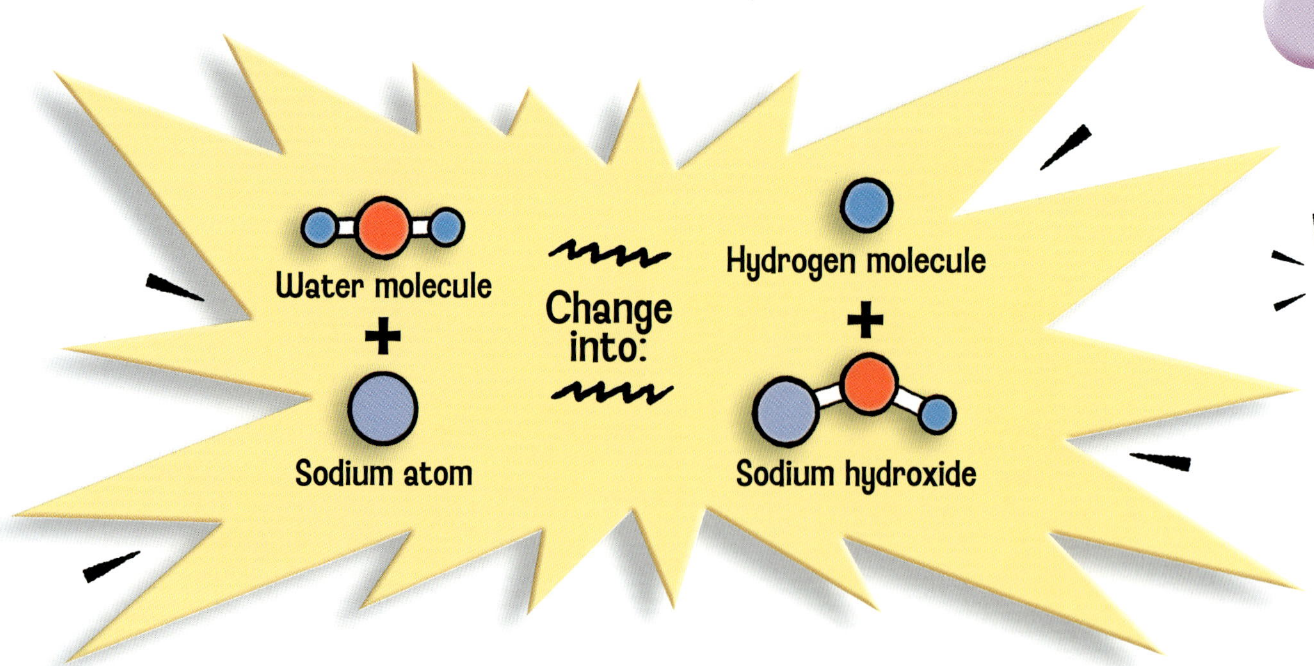

If you count the atoms, you can see they're the same after the reaction, just in different places.

Faster and slower ...

Not all chemical reactions are explosions, though. They can happen more slowly.

Bicarbonate of soda (baking soda) and vinegar react together.

The reaction fizzes and foams, making bubbles of carbon dioxide gas.

Rusting is a chemical reaction, too, but even slower.

Iron atoms react with oxygen atoms in the air, making iron oxide, or rust.

Try it at home!

Chemical reaction experiment

BLOOP BLOOP! SAFETY WARNING!
Make sure you ask an adult to do this with you.

Put 2 teaspoons of bicarbonate of soda into a bottle.

Pour 1/2 cup (118 ml) of vinegar.

Quickly stretch a balloon over the top.

The chemical reaction makes carbon dioxide gas, which fills up the balloon!

Everyday reactions

Chemical reactions are happening all the time.

They happen in cooking when we mix ingredients together.

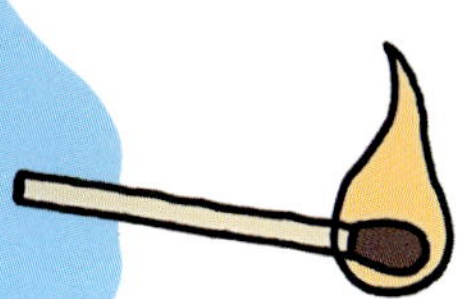

Burning is a kind of chemical reaction too.

And there are constant chemical reactions inside us. It's how your body turns food into energy or into new cells so that you can grow.

Hot and cold

If you put a cup of water in the freezer, it freezes solid. If you put a square of chocolate in your mouth, it melts.

But why?

Because of what the atoms and molecules are doing!

As we all know, things can be solid, like a bar of chocolate …

… or liquid, like water from the tap.

And some things are an invisible gas, like the air we breathe.

You can't see air, but it's definitely there!

In a state!

Scientists call solid, liquid, and gas the **states of matter**. In each state, the atoms and molecules behave differently.

In a solid, they are fixed in place and jiggle to and fro.

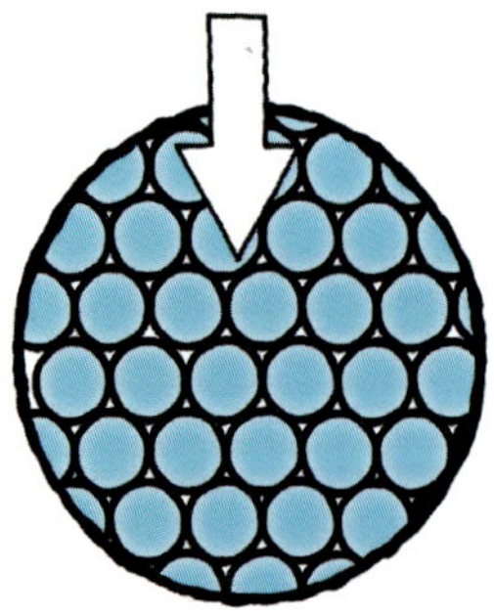

In a liquid, they're farther apart and can slip and slide around.

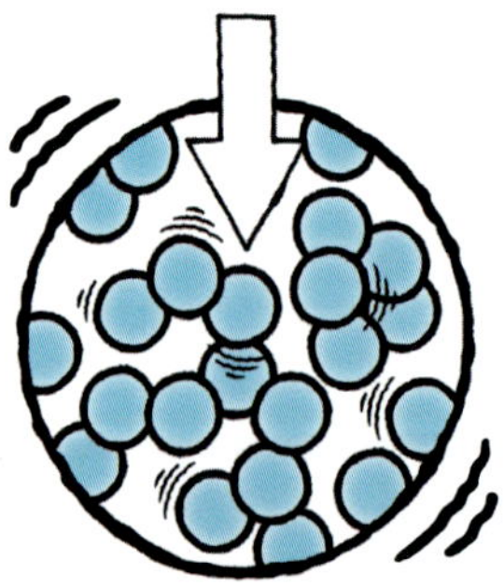

In a gas, they are far apart and whiz around at high speeds.

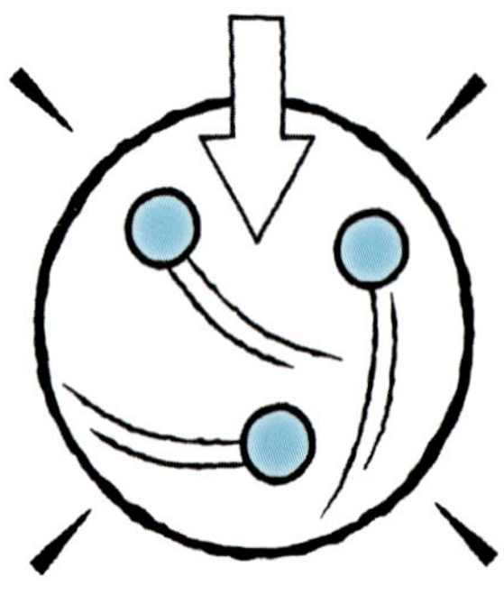

Feeling the heat

Hotter atoms have more energy and move more, and colder atoms move less.

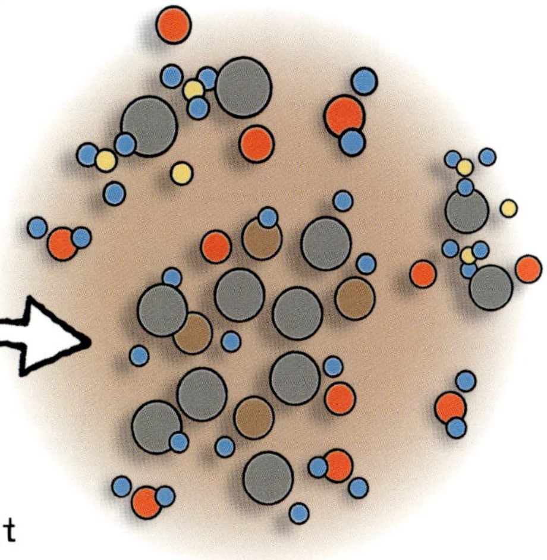

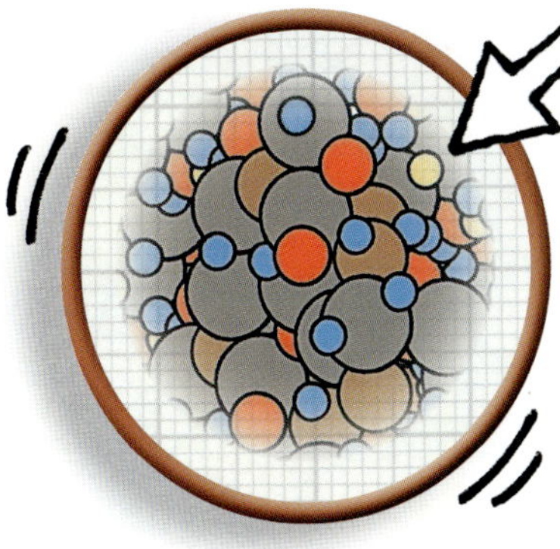

That's why heating up chocolate makes it melt. Heat gives the atoms and molecules more energy, they move faster and spread out, and the solid changes state and becomes a liquid.

In the same way, a liquid can turn into a gas, like when you boil a pan of water and it turns into steam. And the same happens in reverse when things cool down.

Many states

Different materials change state at different temperatures. That's why we have solids, liquids, and gases all around us. At normal temperatures, for example, air is a gas, fruit juice is a liquid, and rock is a solid.

But inside Earth where it's very hot, rock is often liquid.

Lava is melted rock from inside Earth.

How do we know?

Brilliant scientists have used all kinds of experiments to find out how atoms work.

Around 500 BCE

Democritus (see page 4) and other ancient thinkers come up with the idea of atoms.

1869
Mendeleev

As scientists discover more new elements, Russian chemist Dmitri Mendeleev creates an early version of the Periodic Table – after having a dream about it!

1808
Dalton

English scientist John Dalton agrees with Democritus. His "atomic theory" says that since elements react together in different ways, there must be different types of elements. And to be different from each other, elements must have different types of atoms.

1896
The Curies

Marie and Pierre Curie study radioactive elements, which release energy. They realize this energy must be coming from the atoms, which are breaking apart and releasing tiny parts of themselves.

Curium

The element curium was named after the Curies.

1897
Thomson

English scientist J.J. Thomson discovers electrons. He realizes that they must be very small, light parts of atoms.

Thomson worked with cathode ray tubes, which create a beam of electrons.

1908–11
Rutherford

New Zealand–born scientist Ernest Rutherford uses the famous gold foil experiment to discover the parts of an atom.

Gold foil genius

Rutherford's gold foil experiment worked like this.

1. Radiation particles (see pages 20–21) were fired at a sheet of gold foil. This curved screen lit up when a particle hit it.
2. Most of them shot straight through the foil! This showed the gold atoms were mostly empty space.
3. A few bounced off in different directions. This happened when they hit the solid nucleus in the middle of a gold atom.

Rutherford's experiment showed the existence of the nucleus and that atoms are mostly empty.

Splitting the atom

Remember Democritus?
He said you could not cut an atom in two.

But this time, Democritus was … **WRONG!**

We now know that atoms **CAN** be split in two.
However, it's not always a good idea …

Escaping electrons

Electrons can easily escape from atoms. For example, sometimes one atom gives an electron to another atom when they bond together.

Electricity is a flow of electrons that have broken free of their atoms. They can move through a substance, such as a copper wire. Lightning is a flow of electrons too.

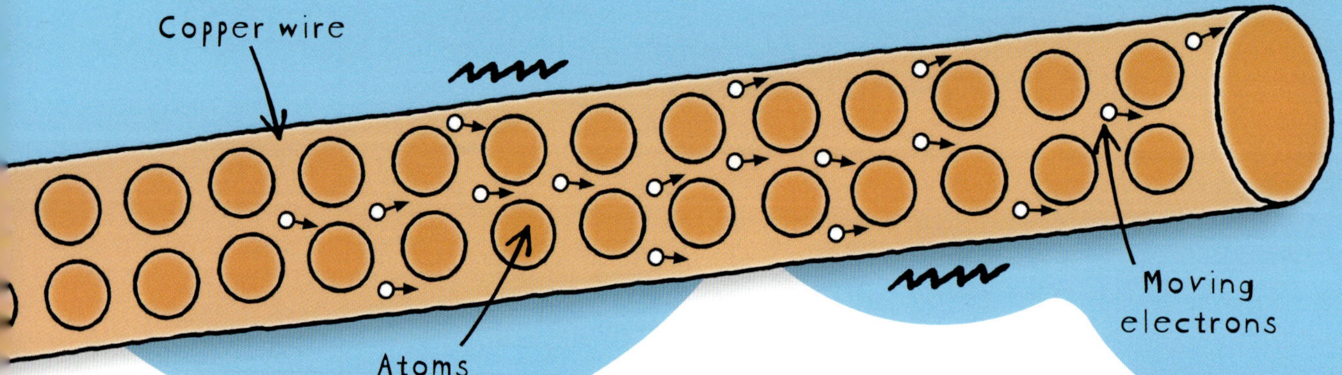

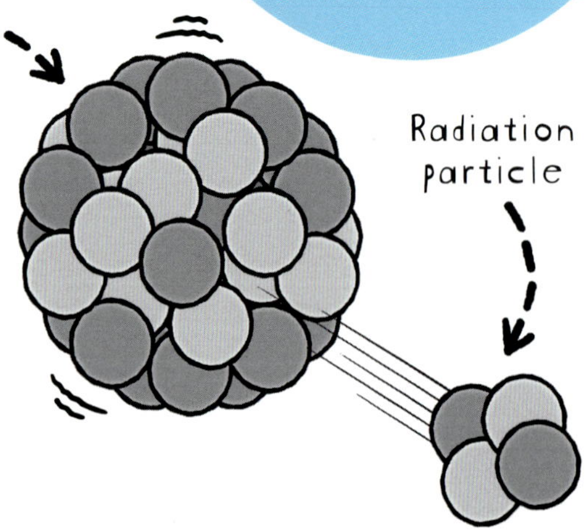

It's radioactive!

When the Curies studied radioactive elements in the 1890s, they found that in some elements, an atom can even lose part of its nucleus, which flies out at high speed.

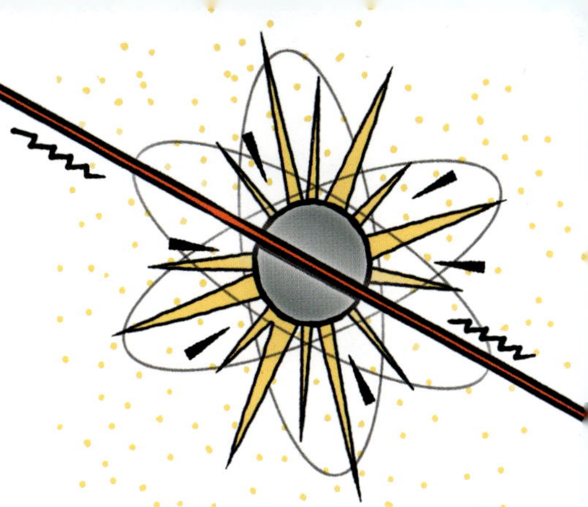

Splitting the atom

After this, other scientists tried to break apart the nucleus of an atom on purpose.

- In 1932, John Cockroft and Ernest Walton split a lithium nucleus by firing a proton at it.
- In 1938, Lise Meitner and Otto Frisch showed how splitting a nucleus, or "nuclear fission," released lots of energy.

A big bang

Soon, people realized this energy could be used to make a big explosion – an atomic bomb, or nuclear weapon. After the Second World War began in 1939, both sides began trying to build one.

Terrible power

Atomic bombs were first used in 1945, when the United States dropped them on Hiroshima and Nagasaki in Japan. Besides killing over 100,000 people right away, they released deadly radiation that killed many more. The effects were so terrible that, so far, atomic bombs have never been used in war again.

Count me out!

At the time, Lise Meitner refused to help build it, saying:

There they are!

Since the 1950s, we've been able to use microscopes to capture images of atoms and molecules.

Early microscopes

When microscopes were first invented, they worked using magnifying lenses made of curved glass. Some microscopes still work like this today.

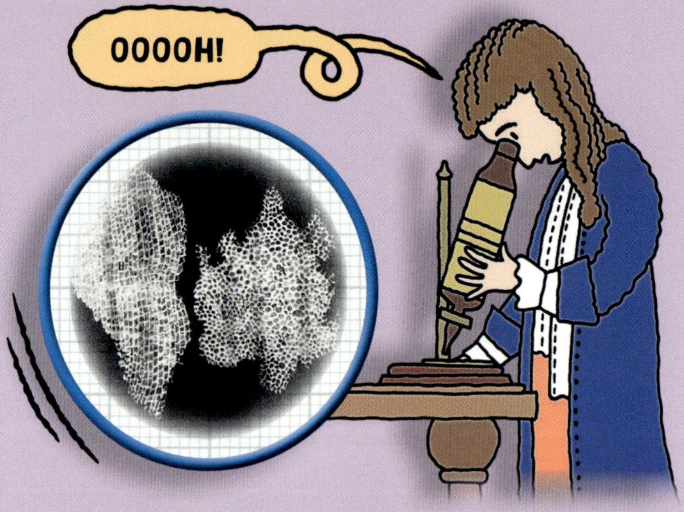

In the 1660s, Robert Hooke discovered cells in cork, using an early microscope.

But atoms are so **TINY** that this type of microscope cannot detect them. We needed a different method. In fact, scientists have invented several ways of doing it!

The first picture

Scientist Erwin Müller and his student Kanwar Bahadur made the first ever image of tungsten atoms in 1955. It looked like this.

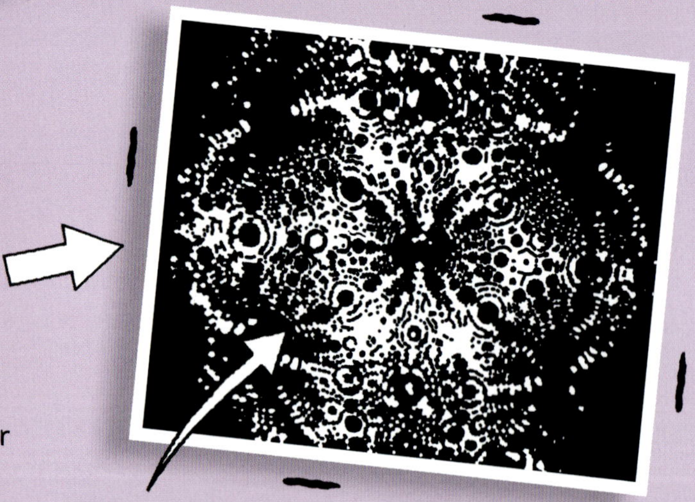

Each dot is one atom.

Müller and Bahadur used a field ion microscope, or FIM, invented by Müller in 1951. It worked by making atoms push particles toward a screen, which showed where the atoms were.

Electron microscopes

Electron microscopes were invented in the 1930s. They fire a beam of electrons at an object. As they bounce off, they reveal the shape of the object.

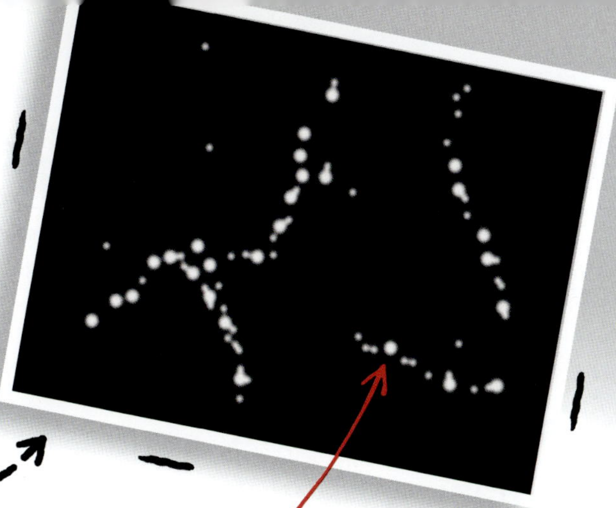

In 1970, a new type of electron microscope was the first to take a picture of atoms.

Atomic force microscopes

The atomic force microscope, or AFM, invented in 1985, gets even closer! It has a tiny sharp tip that can feel the shape of atoms.

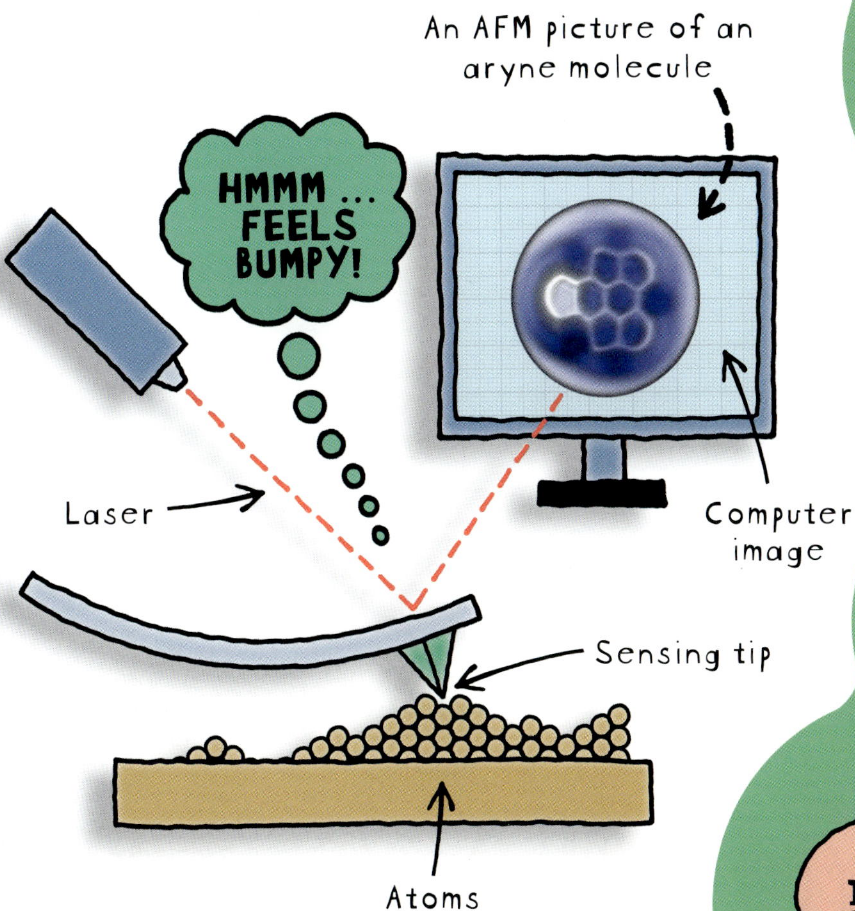

As the tip moves across the atoms, they push against it, making it move. A laser detects the movements, and a computer turns them into an image.

Better microscopes

Scientists are still working on better and better microscopes to look even more closely at atoms. In 2020, they even filmed a video of two atoms in a molecule breaking apart, then joining back together.

Atomic inventions

Scientists have used discoveries about atoms to invent amazing new things ...

Nuclear power

An atomic bomb uses nuclear fission (or splitting the atom) to create a massive explosion. But it can be used in another way too – to supply electricity.

Laser beams

Adding energy to atoms can "excite" their electrons, making them give off light. In 1960, scientists used this knowledge to build the first laser.

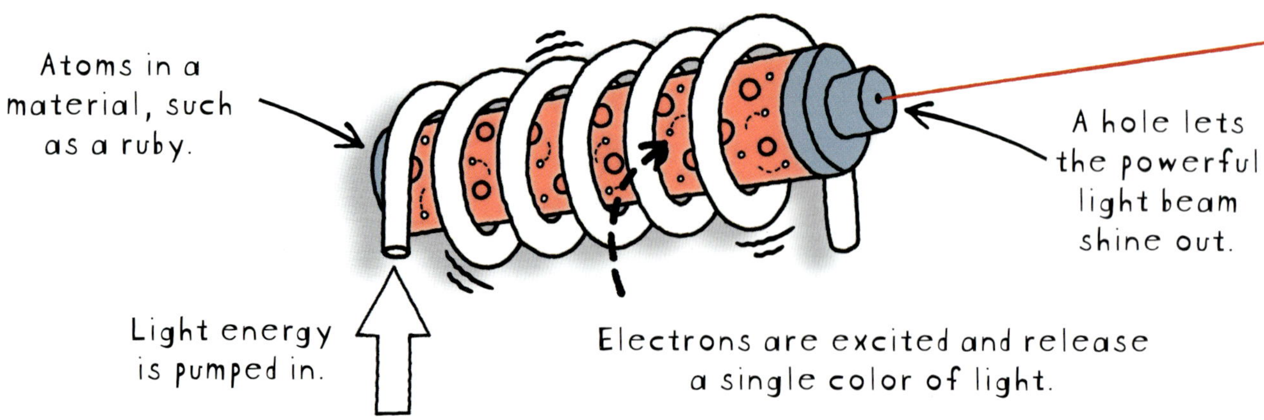

Lasers have many uses: reading barcodes, cutting things, measuring distances, atomic force microscopes (see page 23), and making cat toys!

This high-tech atomic clock uses caesium atoms.

Atomic clock

Atomic clocks were invented in 1949. They zap atoms with energy waves, making them "oscillate," or vibrate, very fast. The vibrations are then used to measure seconds, minutes and hours.

Moving atoms around

Scientists can also use the tip of an atomic force microscope to move and push atoms around.

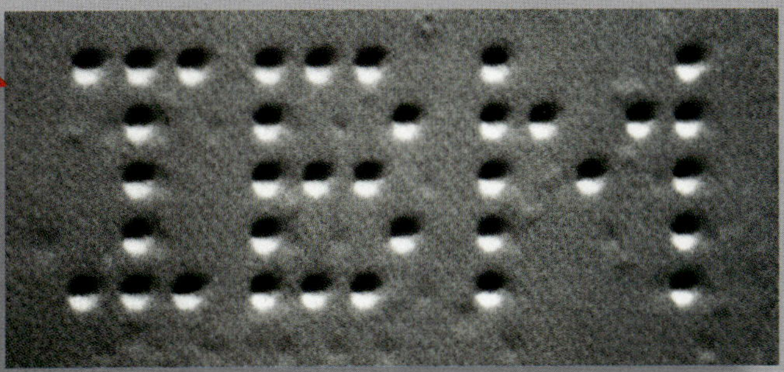

In 1989, staff at tech company IBM used this method to write the IBM logo in atoms.

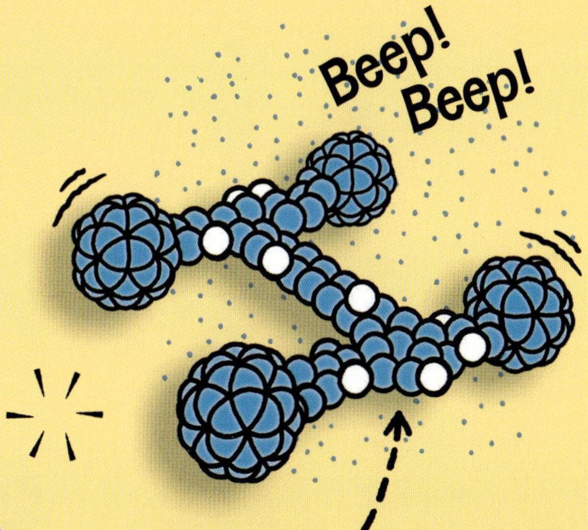

We can now use atoms to build tiny machines like this nanocar, in the new science of nanotechnology. But that's a whole other book!

What are subatomic particles made of?

As you know ...

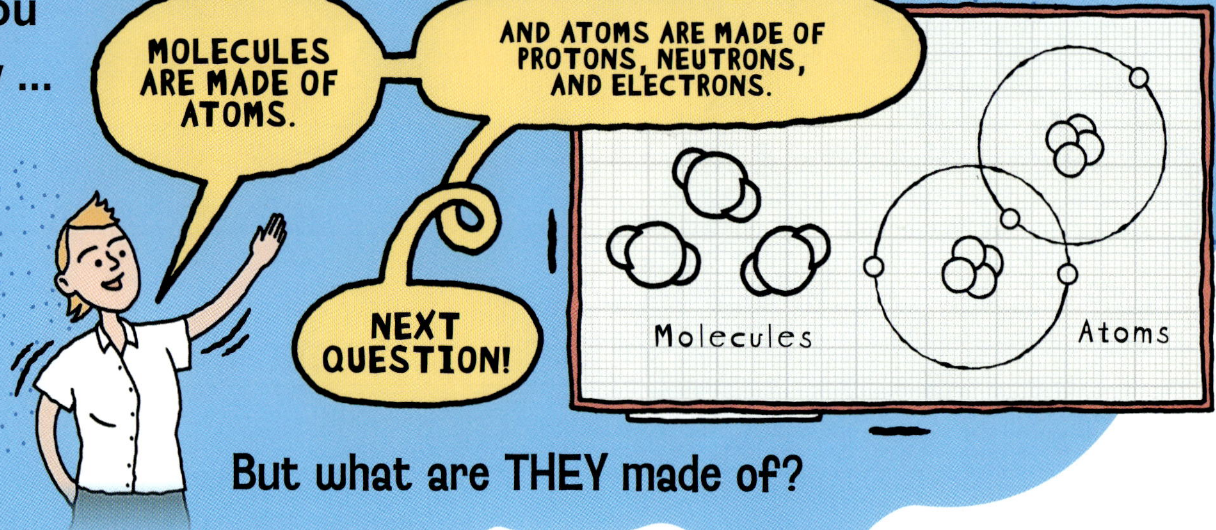

But what are THEY made of?

OK, this is where it gets complicated! Prepare for some **STRANGE SCIENCE** ...

Scientists have come up with various theories – explanations that seem to make sense but aren't yet proven – about this. They think there are lots of even smaller particles, called fundamental particles, that make up the universe.

Atom experiments

Scientists smash atoms apart to look inside them, using machines called particle accelerators, such as the Large Hadron Collider (LHC), a huge, 5-mile (8-km) wide circular underground tunnel, near Geneva, Switzerland.

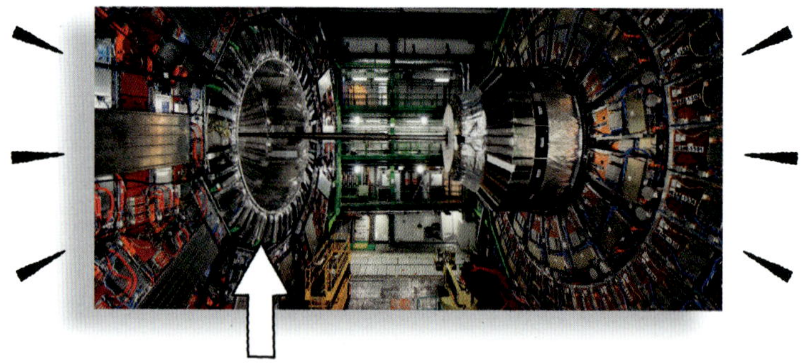

Inside the LHC, powerful machines make tiny particles whiz around the tunnel and smash into other particles, breaking them apart. The bits are too small to see, but machines around the collision detect the paths of particles that fly out.

And the results are ...

Thanks to this work, scientists have discovered a whole range of fundamental particles. They have some very interesting names ...

QUARKS
Up quark
Down quark
Charm quark
Strange quark
Top quark
Bottom quark

LEPTONS
Electron
Muon
Tau
Electron neutrino
Muon neutrino
Tau neutrino

BOSONS
Gluon
Photon
Z boson
W boson
Higgs boson

The neutrons and protons in an atom, for example, are made from quarks, held together by gluons. Electrons are a type of lepton.

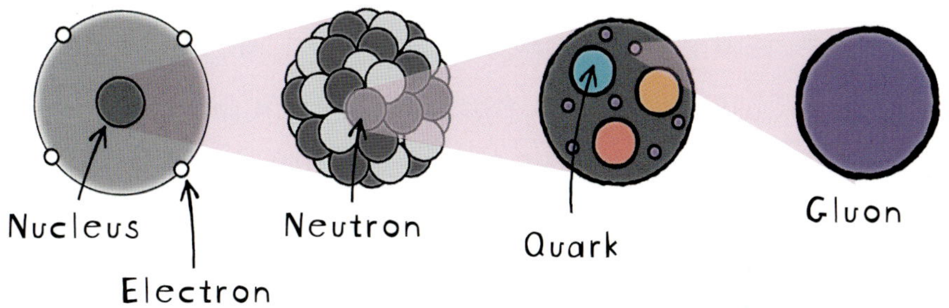

The Standard Model

Today, most scientists agree about this, and it's called the **Standard Model**. It's the best theory we have to explain how matter and energy work.

But what are fundamental particles made of???

Fundamental particles are thought to be the smallest possible particles. They're so small, they are more like single points in space than actual objects.

Quark String

However, some scientists think they are actually tiny, vibrating loops of energy. This is called string theory, and scientists are still debating it.

How tiny?

Atoms are SO tiny, it's almost impossible to imagine. And the parts inside them are even tinier. This page shows how small molecules, atoms, and smaller particles are.

Micro measures

For measuring normal everyday things, we use centimeters, inches, meters, or feet. But these measurements are much too big for measuring objects as small as atoms. Instead, scientists use a much smaller measure, the nanometer.

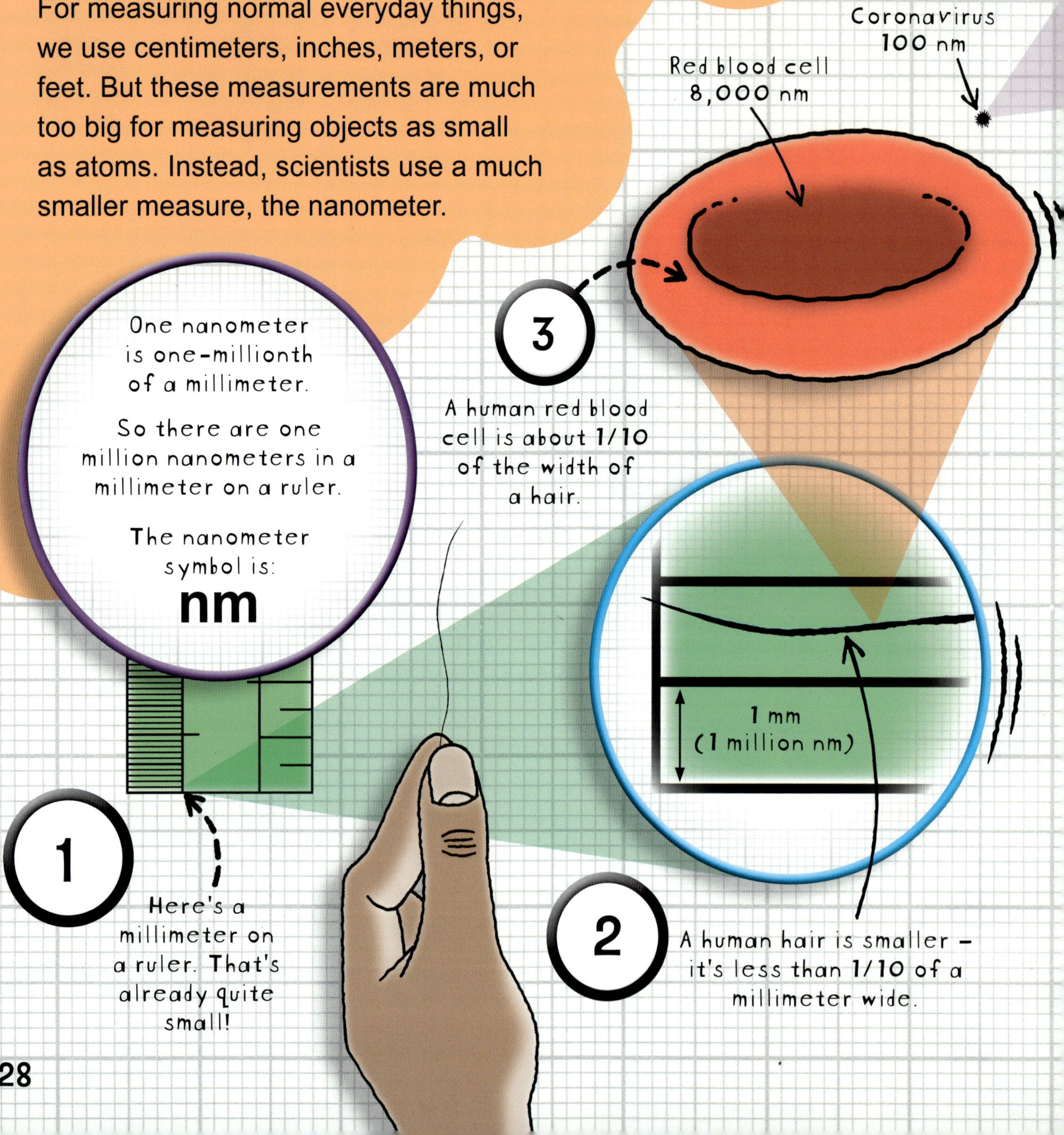

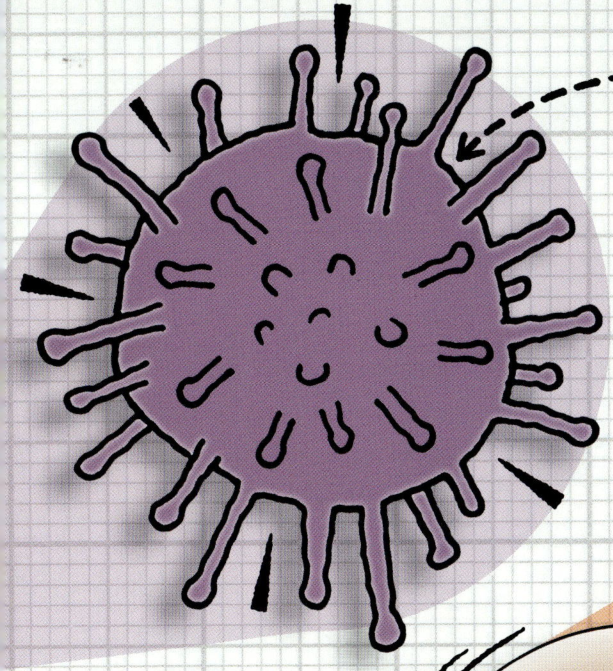

4 A coronavirus, the tiny germ that causes the disease Covid-19, is 1/80 of the width of a red blood cell.

Water molecule 0.3 nm

A water molecule is about 1/300 of the size of a coronavirus.

Oxygen atom 0.2 nm

5 The oxygen atom in a water molecule is about 0.2 nm across – that's one five-millionth of a millimeter.

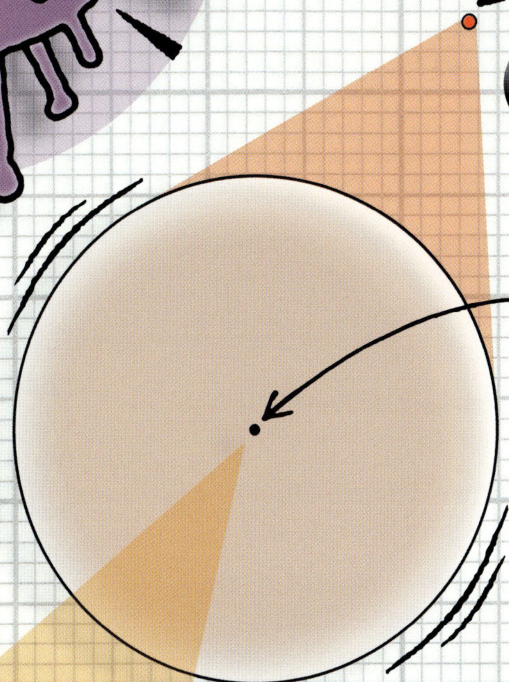

The nucleus of an atom is about 1/100,000 of the size of the atom.

6 Protons and neutrons in an atom's nucleus are about one-millionth of a nanometer across.

Proton 0.000001 nm

Quark

Gluon

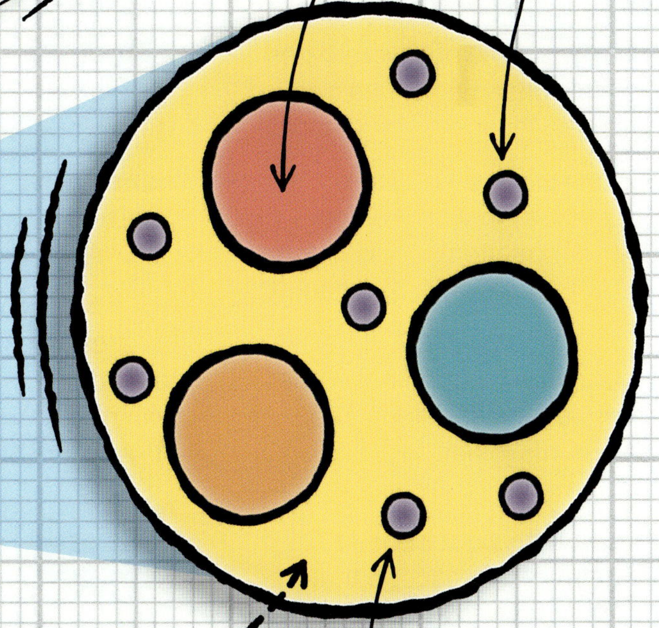

7 And a proton or neutron contains three quarks and several gluons.

Very, very, VERY tiny!!!

Glossary

atomic bomb A very powerful bomb that uses nuclear fission to make an explosion.

atomic clock A clock that uses the vibration of atoms to measure time.

atomic force microscope (AFM) A microscope that uses a fine tip to sense the shapes of atoms.

atomic number A number given to each type of atom, decided by the number of protons in its nucleus.

atomic theory The theory that everything is made up of tiny invisible atoms.

atoms The tiny units that all matter is made of.

bonding The way atoms join together to form molecules.

bosons One of several types of tiny fundamental particles that are thought to form matter.

chemical reaction A process in which atoms rearrange themselves to form new materials when different substances are combined.

compound A material made from atoms of different elements joined together to form molecules.

electron microscope A type of microscope that fires electrons at objects to make an image of them.

electrons Tiny particles that zoom around on the outer edge of atoms.

elements Pure materials made of only one type of atom.

fundamental particles The smallest possible particles of matter, which scientists think make up the particles found in atoms.

laser A device that uses atoms to make a narrow beam of light of a single color.

leptons One of several types of tiny fundamental particles that are thought to form matter.

materials Different types of matter.

matter The stuff that everything is made of.

mixture A material made of different elements or compounds mixed together.

molecules Units of matter made from atoms joined together.

nanometer A tiny unit of measurement, one-millionth of a millimeter long.

nanotechnology An area of science and technology that deals with microscopically small structures and objects.

neutron A type of subatomic particle found in the nucleus of an atom.

nuclear fission Breaking apart the nucleus of an atom to release energy.

nuclear power An energy or electricity supply made by using nuclear fission.

nucleus The solid central part of an atom.

particle A tiny part.

Periodic Table A table or chart showing all the types of atoms and elements.

proton A type of subatomic particle found in the nucleus of an atom.

quarks One of several types of tiny fundamental particles that are thought to form matter.

radioactive elements Elements that release particles or energy waves.

silicon chip A tiny electronic circuit inside a computer.

Standard Model The main scientific theory explaining what matter is made of and how it works.

states of matter The three main states that materials can exist in: solid, liquid, and gas.

string theory A theory that matter is made of very small, string-like vibrating loops.

subatomic particles The tiny particles that atoms are made of.

turbine A device that uses a movement such as a flow of steam to make a wheel spin, which is then used to generate electricity.

Further information

Websites

letstalkscience.ca/educational-resources/backgrounders/introduction-particle-theory-matter

All about particles, with an easy-to-understand video.

www.sciencemuseum.org.uk/objects-and-stories/chemistry/developing-modern-periodic-table-spirals-stars

Science Museum guide to the Periodic Table of the Elements.

education.nationalgeographic.org/resource/a-boy-and-his-atom-the-worlds-smallest-movie/

Watch "A Boy and His Atom," a mini-movie made using atoms.

phet.colorado.edu/sims/html/build-a-molecule/latest/build-a-molecule_en.html

Pick from a selection of atoms and build your own molecules!

Books

See Inside Atoms and Molecules

By Rosie Dickins and Shaw Nielsen (Usborne Books, 2020)

The Element in the Room: Investigating the Atomic Ingredients that Make Up Your Home

By Mike Barfield and Lauren Humphrey (Laurence King, 2018)

The Periodic Table Book: A Visual Encyclopedia of the Elements

By Tom Jackson (Dorling Kindersley, 2017)

Extreme Science: Awesome Matter and Materials

By Jon Richards and Rob Colson (Wayland, 2020)

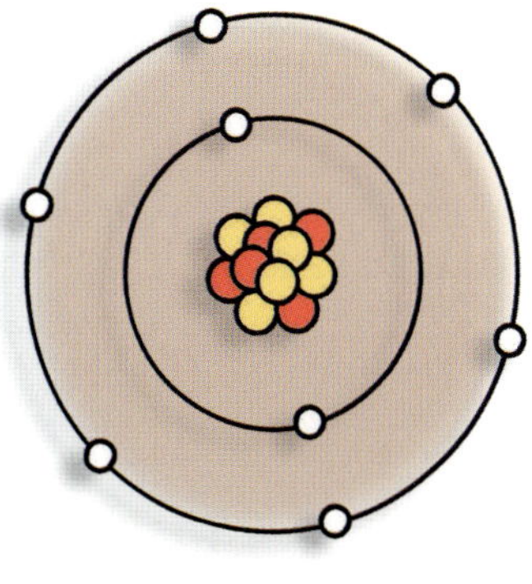

Every effort has been made by the Publishers to ensure that the websites in this book are suitable for children, that they are of the highest educational value, and that they contain no inappropriate or offensive material. However, because of the nature of the Internet, it is impossible to guarantee that the contents of these sites will not be altered. We strongly advise that Internet access is supervised by a responsible adult.

Index